Help I'm Creating a Nonprofit

By
Jasmine Baker

Table of Contents

Introduction

Creating a non-profit organization is a costly and time-consuming endeavor. Before starting a non-profit, it's a good idea to think about the attrition rate. A huge majority of people who form non-profits eventually conclude that the rewards aren't worth the effort and abandon their altruistic goals. Creating a nonprofit, like any successful business, takes a lot of effort. The road to success is paved with perseverance and resolution, and the rewards are well worth the effort. Follow along as I discuss some suggestions for reducing the chances that your nonprofit will become one of the failures.

You've decided to start a nonprofit organization to make a difference in the world, and now you need to figure out how to get started. A nonprofit requires a lot of work, but not so much that almost anyone can accomplish it. However, there are several crucial procedures to consider before getting started. Follow along below, and I'll give you seven helpful hints to get you started in the right direction. When properly implemented, these suggestions will aid in the success of your nonprofit.

So you're considering creating a nonprofit organization. Maybe you're enthusiastic about a certain cause or seeking for a long-term solution to aid a specific neighborhood. Obviously, the first thing that comes to mind is: how can I form a nonprofit? It's a major step, and you'll need to be well-versed in a variety of legal, financial, and program-related startup details.

This guide provides thorough information and resources to anyone thinking about establishing a nonprofit organization.

Chapter One: Why A Nonprofit?

What Is a Nonprofit Organization?

Nonprofits are organizations that serve a social purpose, such as public charities, foundations, churches, fraternal organizations, and chambers of commerce. They cover a wide range of structures, including non-governmental organizations, or NGOs.

Non-governmental organizations are more likely to take on broader issues, typically on a global basis. According to the National Center for Charitable Statistics, there are over 1.5 million nonprofit organizations in the United States (NCCS).

A nonprofit organization (NPO), also known as a non-profit entity, not-for-profit organization, or nonprofit institution, is a legal body that is founded and operated for a collective, public, or social benefit, as opposed to an entity that operates as a business and seeks to create a profit for its owners.

Nonprofit organizations exist to improve the quality of life for others on a community, local, state, national, and even global scale. These organizations are dedicated to the development of the public interest rather than private or financial gain.

Nonprofit Organizations and the Laws that Apply to Them

Nonprofit organizations are governed by both state and federal law, but they lack a statutory definition in the United

States. Most states allow nonprofits to incorporate for any reason as long as it is lawful and no earnings are paid to the members.

The nonprofit's objective must, however, be approved by the Internal Revenue Code in order to receive tax-exempt status and other benefits (IRC).

A nonprofit organization's funds must be put to good use in order to achieve its objective. Paid employees, on the other hand, can be hired to oversee the activities of the organization.

Getting Started with a Nonprofit

When forming a nonprofit organization, it's important to first determine its mission. What are your goals for this organization? This might range from forming a neighborhood group to promoting local artists' work to addressing significant concerns like homelessness, health care, and hunger.

You may come up with a meaningful name, assess whether you'll be able to petition for tax-exempt status, and look for suitable board members once you've defined the organization's mission. If you're interested in becoming a 501(c)(3) tax-exempt organization, you should talk to a tax professional.

Developing a Mission Statement for a Nonprofit Organization

A nonprofit organization's mission statement explains why it exists. It should consist of the following components:

The market or target audience that you intend to reach out to.

What kind of service or product do you intend to provide in this market?

These are the characteristics of the company that set it apart from other product and service providers in that market.

Articles of Incorporation

To start a nonprofit organization, you must first submit articles of incorporation with the state in which you intend to operate. The purpose clause should be given special attention. This area will be scrutinized by the IRS to see if your group meets the requirements for tax-exempt status. They also offer suggested language for this section for companies to use.

For your articles of incorporation, you can get a template from the Secretary of State's website. If you need to provide further information, you can attach extra pages. You should, for example, include information about your organization's mission and goals. Your organization bylaws can benefit from the descriptive wording you develop for the articles.

Why A Nonprofit?

Tax-exempt status with the IRS and personal liability protection for employees are two benefits of non-profit organizations. Running a nonprofit organization, on the other hand, might be challenging. If they don't fully comprehend what it takes to have a successful career in the nonprofit sector, some organizers can soon burn out.

A nonprofit organization (NPO) is one that obtains commodities, donations, sponsorships, and services in order to carry out its objective. The objective of a nonprofit is frequently to help the community through groups such as these:

- Clubs
- Associations
- Churches
- Chamber of commerce
- Nonprofits may also support and promote a social cause, such as:
- Humanitarian assistance
- Disease research
- Education funding

Nonprofit organizations differ from for-profit organizations in that for-profit organizations were created with the intention of sharing earnings with their investors and shareholders. Incorporation is the first step toward becoming a tax-exempt charity entity for a firm that wants to become a nonprofit.

When a nonprofit organization obtains tax-exempt status, it is no longer required to pay income taxes on funds or gifts received as part of its fundraising efforts. It will also not disperse any of its profits to its members, directors, or executives. A nonprofit organization can be created in a variety of ways, including as a:

- Foundation
- Corporation
- Partnership
- Individual business

Working for a nonprofit organization has a lot of advantages. Employees may have access to group life insurance, health insurance, and pension plans if the NPO is a business.

Section 501(c)(3) of the Internal Revenue Code (c)

Nonprofits' tax-exempt status is defined by Internal Revenue Code Section 501(c). To be tax-exempt, an organization must be organized and operated only for the following purposes:

- Charity
- Science
- Education
- Religion
- Literary
- Public safety is paramount.
- Sports for amateurs
- Animal Cruelty Prevention
- Child cruelty prevention

Boards or members can run non-profits. Their corporate structure can contain both paid and unpaid employees. One of the following should be the focus of a NPO.

- Health
- Visual and performing arts
- Concerns about the environment
- Advocacy for victims and their families
- Services related to the culture

Nonprofit revenue cannot be received by private shareholders or individuals.

The Benefits of Nonprofit Organizations

Nonprofit organizations have a number of benefits, including:

Life without End

A nonprofit organization can continue to exist as long as its mission is relevant and it can generate revenue. This is true even if the organization's founder has left or passed away. More than 1,500 years ago, Japan established the world's oldest nonprofit organization. Because the entity is distinct from the person, it can continue to exist indefinitely. This can make these businesses appealing to donors who want to support a cause that will last a long time.

On a Larger Scale Organization

Setting up a nonprofit around your chosen cause can help you to establish a larger team or program and, in turn, have a larger influence if you have a mission or are dedicated to making the world a better place.

Personal Liability Insurance

In the event of a lawsuit, one of the key benefits of founding a nonprofit organization is that employees will not be personally liable for corporate debts or injury awards. If a lawsuit is filed or the business defaults on its debts, the business and its assets will be held liable.

A nonprofit will operate legally as a limited liability organization after it is established. This helps to keep business and personal assets distinct. Though NPO owners and founders would be shielded from indebtedness, they would not be protected from illegal or responsible conduct in which they engage. Directors and members are obligated to fulfill their job tasks in the nonprofit's best interest, and if they don't, they can be held accountable.

Even if your organization is protected from liability, it's still a smart idea to have commercial liability insurance to cover you in scenarios that aren't covered by incorporated laws.

Exemption from paying taxes

Nonprofit organizations are excluded from corporation taxation as well as income taxation at the federal, state, and local levels. This manner, you can reinvest all of your profits in the company to expand its offerings.

Tax-deductible donations to non-profits might make financial gifts to these organizations more appealing.

Limitation of Liability

Starting a nonprofit organization can be less risky than starting a small business as a lone proprietor or partner. States throughout the country are implementing legislation that allows limited liability charities to be formed, according to Nonprofit Law Blog. Limited liability provides legal protection to business owners from creditors and other stakeholders.

Although most nonprofit finance is obtained through grants and donations that do not require repayment, a new organization may nonetheless require debt financing. This can be especially risky for a company that isn't primarily concerned with creating a viable business plan. This new nonprofit organization promises to provide social entrepreneurs with the security they need to go out and try new structures and services.

Leaving a Mark

Running a high-impact charity organization can give you a place in history as someone who made a difference in the world, not just as someone who amassed cash. Rather than focusing simply on their own company, successful social entrepreneurs are actively involved in growing and sustaining their field of impact as a whole. Some people believe that creating a real difference in people's lives or in the natural world is more important than building long-term profitable businesses.

Separation of entity status

A nonprofit corporation (or LLC) exists in its own right. It can enter into contracts on its own behalf, sue and be sued in its own name, and is accountable for all contractual and other responsibilities. If a contract is breached in an informal or non-statutory nonprofit, the person engaging in the deal in his or her own name may be held accountable.

Discounts from the United States Postal Service

Nonprofits that are tax-exempt are often eligible for bulk mail discounts.

Credibility

A nonprofit corporation may have more established credibility than an individual or individuals attempting to achieve a nonprofit goal on their own. Because of this reputation, donors may prefer to donate to nonprofit organizations.

Professional registered agent

A registered agent is required for statutory nonprofits such as corporations and limited liability companies. This allows them to appoint a professional registered agent, which assists in the correct handling of essential, time-sensitive court documents that will be served if the nonprofit is sued.

Pursue your dreams

Individuals often start charity organizations to pursue a passion, whether it's because they lost a loved one to a sickness, were in an abusive relationship, want to mentor young children, or want to raise environmental awareness. As a charity leader, you have the opportunity to pursue your passion while also sharing it with others who share it.

Positive Participation in the Community

Nonprofit organizations are established to serve communities by offering resources and support. Each nonprofit contributes to the overall growth of its community, from art centers that educate children how to draw and produce pottery sculptures to groups that help entrepreneurs launch their enterprises.

The Disadvantages of Forming a Nonprofit Organization

Some of the drawbacks of establishing a statutory nonprofit corporation is listed below (or LLC).

Expenses

Forming a statutory nonprofit corporation necessitates filing documents with the state's business entity filing office, which necessitates the payment of filing costs. In most states, you'll also have to pay annual fees to the state. A professional registered agent is also advised, but there is a fee for that as well.

Obligations for ongoing compliance

Statutory nonprofits must also follow the requirements of the statute under which they were established. This can include things like publishing an annual report, drafting bylaws (or an operating agreement), keeping specific books and records, and reporting to the state when the firm undergoes significant changes.

Management oversight

Nonprofit statutes, particularly nonprofit company laws, govern how a nonprofit is to be run. For example, the law may impose requirements such as a board of directors, regular meetings, quorums, minutes, and other compliance requirements that informal charities are exempt from.

There will be no political campaigning or lobbying

Lobbying and political activities are restricted for tax-exempt NGOs, which can limit their capacity to advocate for their interests.

Paperwork

In order to maintain its active and exempt status, a nonprofit must keep extensive records and submit annual filings to the state and IRS by certain deadlines.

Control is shared

Personal control is limited for those who start nonprofits, despite their desire to shape and govern their creations. A nonprofit organization is bound by rules and regulations, including its own bylaws and articles of incorporation. In some states, a nonprofit is required to have a board of directors, who are the only people who can elect or appoint policy-making officials.

Four Important Factors Affecting Nonprofit Success

A nonprofit's success can be influenced by a variety of things. Is it hundreds or thousands? It's difficult to know where to stop once we start listing everything that can determine whether a nonprofit succeeds or fails.

Instead, let's look at four elements that we know are present in every successful charity organization 100 percent of the time. Your organization's potential for success is enormous if you can develop the four characteristics listed below.

1. A board of directors that is well-informed, passionate, and involved

Is each member of your board of directors well-versed in the following topics?

The importance of the nonprofit sector in our communities' well-being.

The importance of the board of directors in the organization's performance, as well as the roles and responsibilities of individual board members.

The organization's mission as well as the need in your town.

Why did he or she opt to join the board as an individual?

Some of these topics may require training for your board members. They may not be fully knowledgeable when they join your organization, but you must have a plan in place to help them learn more.

Of course, passionate means that the board member actually cares about the organization, its objective, and the people it is responsible for. The organization's mission should be one of the board members' top two or three personal concerns.

When a board member comes to meetings prepared, engages in the conversation, asks questions, and holds everyone accountable, including himself or herself, he or she is engaged. Board members who are actively involved in the organization's events and activities are more likely to advocate for it.

2. A board member-to-board member relationship based on mutual respect, sincerity, and open communication.

The foundation for open and honest communication among board members is trust. Members must be able to express their opinions and share their knowledge without fear of personal or professional retaliation from other board members. This open communication will improve the board's work results and expedite the process.

3. A knowledgeable and devoted team leader

To achieve the organization's objective, the board of directors and the chief staff person must work together as a team. As a result, the board must take the time to carefully pick the best applicant for the role and then work to assist that individual. The organization can move forward with tremendous efficacy if the board is well-informed, passionate, and involved, as well as if the staff is strong.

4. A relationship between the main staff person and all board members is based on mutual respect, candor, and open communication.

The board and the top staff person must share the same level of trust that exists among board members. This trust will lead to open dialogue about important issues, which will help the company move forward. The main staff person should feel safe approaching board members with the words "This is what keeps me up at night..." and anticipate a substantive discussion without fear of being judged or punished.

Most businesses must struggle to develop these four crucial success elements; they are rarely accomplished without a strategy for doing so. The organization will be successful if the board and senior staff realize the value of each and want to attain them.

Why Do So Many Non-Profit Organizations Fail?

With over 1.5 million tax-exempt organizations in the United States alone, it's no surprise that thousands of them collapse every year. According to Forbes, half of all businesses will fail within the first year. Other statistics show it's lower, with the National Centre for Charitable Statistics estimating it to be closer to 30%.

In any case, the data shows that no one can be certain of success, even in normal circumstances. The topic of why a nonprofit fails is just as essential as the question of how one may have navigated a safe road to success.

It's a sad reality that some NGOs fail, but by recognizing these pitfalls, we can all better adapt, endure, and prosper.

Here are the first five challenges to solve, all of which I've seen and even experienced in my own charity career.

1. Inability to keep up with technological advances

Stagnation might be indicated by a failure to keep up with the latest innovations. We can't all be Bill Gates, but we can at least acknowledge the importance of technological advancements. Too many NGOs feel that if they have a good mission, they will be fine. The difficulty is that others will be watching, and ignoring technology and online growth improves your chances of being among the thirty to fifty percent.

If you have any questions about what this implies in your area, reach out to those in the tech industry. Experts are frequently eager to assist good causes and will offer information about developments and opportunities.

2. A reluctance to invest in unappealing infrastructure

When it comes to establishing their usefulness to early backers, new NGOs generally hesitate to invest in anything other than front-line services. This commendable intention, however, leads to major complications down the road. Eventually, the backstage activities that support long-term growth become underdeveloped. This results in stagnation and, as a result, a reduction in operating scope.

It's logical to believe that contributors want to know that every dollar goes to the front lines. However, how can you dig coal out of the ground without first investing in the machinery, manpower, pit head, and train that will transport it?

To be a successful nonprofit, you must focus on both infrastructure and service delivery; the two are intertwined. It is longevity that is important.

Your contributors will value long-term investment as much as they value immediate gratification from completing the core purpose.

3. Failure of the founder

This is a problem that both businesses and organizations face. When a single individual is in charge of an organization, it might be difficult for fresh ideas to propagate.

The founder's syndrome in nonprofits is difficult to overcome. Democracy is uncommon in businesses and organizations. "Just do what I say!" is frequently used as an unspoken and ineffective policy.

As a result of this, you may experience the following side effects:

Potentially talented employees and volunteers are being scared away.

It becomes more difficult to put new ideas into action.

Structures that are obvious to others are ignored because the person in charge refuses to see their importance.

Donors can tell when a nonprofit is tainted by one person's ego. They are more inclined to desire to see the purpose realized than the founder's ego inflated.

When a forceful founder starts to believe the mission is the same as themselves, they can destroy their own efforts. The truth is that there will be a large number of people willing and able to help a good cause, each with their own set of skills and passion.

Founder syndrome places a throne where a round table should be and a chauffeur where a team bus should be.

4. Drilling a hole in the center

This occurs when a nonprofit organization does not create a clear set of ethical principles from the start.

Even if you only have one person on staff, having a clear mission statement, code of conduct, and clear concepts about what the nonprofit stands for and what standards are expected is critical.

We're all working with sensitive financial, ethical, and personal data. It is a moral and legal obligation to ensure that everyone you contact or hire is compliant with your fundamental code of conduct.

There must be some kind of assessment to ensure that these requirements are followed. The most precious asset you have is your nonprofit's reputation. It is non-refundable, so keep it safe! It's not an afterthought, as I've seen some people believe. It's a lot easier to hire the proper people up front than it is to get rid of the wrong people later.

5. The small details count

When you walk into a doctor's office, you anticipate a specific environment, a certain level of care, and a certain demeanor.

You make snap judgments if they reach out to examine you with dirty fingernails and stains all over their clothes.

You'll feel that they weren't as professional as you wanted, regardless of how high the level of care is or how skilled the physician is. At every level of its development, your nonprofit will be subjected to the same superficial assessments.

Investing in the minor aspects, such as professional communication, a logo, and an up-to-date website with intriguing content, may make a big difference.

Keeping the tiny details in good order isn't an issue of financial resources. It only takes a conscious effort to go above and beyond when necessary. It will be recognized, and it will attract attention and support in your direction.

Even when organizations fail, other ventures emerge with new purposes to accomplish. It's just as important to learn from those who tried and failed as it is to examine how others succeeded. In this way, we may continue to grow and make a difference in the world, which is ultimately what matters.

Resources

Associate Membership
Free membership level that includes access to a library with archived issues of Nonprofit World and Funding Alert, a subscription to GrantStation Insider, and access to the Nonprofit Careers job listings.

Book Reviews
Read more than 10 years of book reviews from Nonprofit World magazine. Reviewed books include diverse areas of interest for nonprofit leaders and managers.

Free Articles
provided is a collection of more than 30 hand-picked articles from the Nonprofit World library. Articles can be downloaded without registration, and represent a wide variety of focus areas.

Fundraising Guide
The Society's guide to finding your hidden assets and matching them to proven fundraising strategies. Includes steps and exercises that will help you to mine your organization's resources.

Job Listings
Find jobs, board positions, and volunteer opportunities in the nonprofit sector. 100% free for job seekers. Free postings for Society members, and just $50/post for non-members.

Nonprofit Links
Find new resources for funding information, look for new volunteers, and learn about the latest technology available to nonprofits at some of the most useful online resources.

National Directory
This National Directory helps nonprofits to find leading companies that offer a wide range of products and services for the nonprofit sector.

Sample Documents & Handouts
A collection of samples, templates, handouts and other documents intended to provide you with a starting point and save you from reinventing the wheel.

Social Networks
Reach out to other nonprofit professionals using some of the most popular social networking platforms, including Facebook, LinkedIn, Twitter, and Yahoo.

Starting A Nonprofit (FAQ)
Find answers to some of the most commonly asked questions, links to recommended reading, and relevant articles from past issues of Nonprofit World.

Funding Opportunities for U.S.-Based Individuals

Giving Kitchen—providing emergency relief grants for food industry workers in Georgia and compiling a Stability Network, a list of organizations providing food industry workers support state-by-state

USA.Gov—Summarizing the CARES Act, and how it can support your day-to-day needs due to the effects of COVID-19

Creative Capital—listing local and national grants for artists and arts professionals affected by COVID-19

Sweet Relief—Accepting applications for musicians to support vital living expenses and offset the financial burden of canceled events

PFund— Providing support to the LGBTQIA community is accepting applications for their COVID-19 response fund on a rolling basis. The first round of funding is prioritizing people particularly impacted by the COVID-19 pandemic.

Caress + IFundWomen of Color—Providing grant funding and additional resources to the womxn BIPOC entrepreneur community.

Nonprofit Statistics You Should Know

Whether they are established as philanthropic institutions, civic leagues, social welfare organizations, or social advocacy groups, nonprofits can be a force for good in the world. They can work on a wide range of problems, including healthcare, animal welfare, and arts and culture. Nonprofits provide comfort that there are people willing to help those in need in a society where societal problems have been exacerbated by the pandemic.

Readers can learn about general nonprofit statistics, financials, and donor and volunteer demographics and behavior in this compilation of nonprofit statistics. Those who want to learn more about them can look through the data to have a better understanding of the nonprofit sector. Those working in the nonprofit sector, on the other hand, may use the information presented here, together with their preferred donor management software, to efficiently administer their organizations.

Nonprofit Statistics in General

Nonprofits' earnings are frequently reinvested in the organization to help it realize its core goal. Total revenue and program revenue for NGOs in the United States have surpassed $1 billion in the last two years. In fact, according to nonprofit statistics, 2019 was one of the most generous years in US history. On the other hand, charitable giving in the United Kingdom has also reached billions of pounds.

There are almost two million nonprofit organizations and 501(c)(3) charities in the United States. Churches and religious groups are the most common type of nonprofit in the United States, followed by civic, social, and economic organizations. In the meantime, there are approximately 180,000 charities in the United Kingdom.

The Value of Nonprofits

The entire revenue from NGOs in 2019 was above $84.7 billion, according to a nonprofit industry overview. This is a 5% increase over the previous year's figures. (2019, The Nonprofit Times).

- In 2019, the largest charitable organizations in the United States generated $21.4 billion in program revenue. (2019, The Nonprofit Times).
- In 2019, the largest NGOs in the United States generated $21.4 billion in program revenue. (2019, The Nonprofit Times).
- Nine of the largest nonprofits in the United States reported investment revenue of more than $100 million in 2019. (2019, the Nonprofit Times).
- In England and Wales, total income and endowments for charity totaled £77,825,024,292. (England & Wales Charity Commission, 2021).
- In the United States, charitable donations by individuals, bequests, foundations, and businesses totaled $449.64 billion in 2019. 2019 was one of the most generous years in the history of charitable giving. (2020, United States of America).

Nonprofit Organizations by Geography and Cause:

In the United States, there are 1.5 million tax-exempt charities. (National Academy of Sciences, National Academy of Engineering, National Academy of Sciences, National Academy of Sciences,

There will be 1.8 million nonprofit organizations in the United States by 2020. In contrast, the United States has 1.7 million active nonprofit organizations, including numerous categories of NGOs and 501(c)(3) charities. 2020 (Cause Intelligence)"

- Meanwhile, there are 1.4 million registered charities and 501(c)(3) NGOs that accept tax-deductible contributions. 2020 (Cause Intelligence) "
- Churches, schools, and foundations account for over 40% of all nonprofits in the United States. Civil, social, and corporate engagement organizations, on the other hand, account for 15% of the total. Meanwhile, 7% of the funds go to human services and another 7% to cultural and humanities organizations. 2020 (Cause Intelligence) "
- Religious groups and churches are the most common nonprofits in the United States. Religious groups account for 16.7% of all nonprofits, with 300,747 in total. In second place, with 248,253 organizations, or 13.8 percent of all charities, schools and other educational institutions are in second place. Foundations and grant making organizations, which account for 165,031 nonprofits or 9.2% of all nonprofits, are in third position. 2020 (Cause Intelligence) "

- There are 106,000 charitable organizations in Texas, or about one for every 4,000 residents. (National Academy of Sciences, National Academy of Engineering, National Academy of Sciences, National Academy of Sciences,
- In the United States, there are over 47,000 charities dedicated to women's and girls' issues. They represent only 3.3 percent of all charitable organizations and 1.6 percent of total charitable giving.(Women's Philanthropy Institute of the IUPI, 2019)
- As of May 10, 2021, England and Wales have a total of 185,241 charities. (England & Wales Charity Commission, 2021).

Nonprofit Financial Statistics:

According to nonprofit statistics acquired from the top 100 organizations in the United States, public support revenues account for a significant portion of their budgets. According to another survey, NGOs got an average of $700 in gifts from contributors, whereas typical internet donations were roughly $170. Nonprofits nevertheless spend billions on administrative costs, even with these gifts. They must additionally account for COVID-related expenses due to the ongoing pandemic, which can raise their operating costs. As a result, NGOs must master the art of fundraising and make use of cutting-edge technologies like fundraising software.

- Public funding supports 10% of the largest nonprofit groups in the United States. This amounts to $46.6 billion in 2019. In comparison to 2018, this figure increased by 3.43 percent.(2019, The Nonprofit Times).

- In 2019, the largest organizations in the United States spent $79.7 billion on expenses. This is a 4.2 percent increase over last year.(National Academy of Sciences, National Academy of Engineering, National Academy of Sciences, National Academy of Sciences,

- Administrative costs for the largest organizations in the United States totaled $6.27 billion in 2019. Fundraising expenses, on the other side, totaled over $4 billion, while program expenses totaled $69.5 billion. (National Academy of Sciences, National Academy of Engineering, National Academy of Sciences, National Academy of Sciences,

- In 2020, non-profits got an average gift of $737. In 2019, however, the average gift amount was $617. (2020, Blackbaud)

- In 2020, the average online donation amount for all nonprofit subsectors was $177. K-12 NGOs received the highest average online donation of $1,640. Health care ($403), higher education ($387), and public and societal benefits ($241) follow. (2020, Blackbaud)

- In Missouri, nonprofits reported an average increase in COVID-related expenses of $302,417 per organization. Nonprofits in Pennsylvania, on the other hand, reported $95.3 million in higher operational expenditures as a result of the epidemic. (Project for Nonprofit Education Survey, 2021)

Volunteer Statistics

In terms of volunteer demographics, one study discovered that people under the age of 55 are more likely to volunteer. Volunteers in the United Kingdom, on the other hand, are between the ages of 65 and 74. Furthermore, the majority of volunteers in the United Kingdom participate in activities at least once a year. However, while it is still possible to assist during the epidemic, over half of those who have volunteered have decided to reduce their engagement.

- People under the age of 55, according to 44% of nonprofit supporters, are more willing to volunteer. People aged 55 and up are more willing to volunteer, according to 38% of respondents. (2020, Freewill)
- Nonprofit supporters are more likely to update their will, according to 26% of them. Meanwhile, 14% said they are unlikely to change their minds.(2020, Freewill)
- Hearing from charitable organizations benefits 46% of supporters. On the other hand, 21% indicated they had not observed. (2020, Freewill)
- Seventy percent of charitable donors prefer to be contacted by email. Physical mail is preferred by 7%, while social media is preferred by 6%. (2020, Freewill)
- During the pandemic, 47% of volunteers said they would cut back or cease volunteering completely. Only 17% stated they would increase their volunteer time. (2020, Fidelity Charitable)
- 6% of young Americans said they have personally volunteered for a cause or group. Another 6% stated that they did so virtually or online. (Cause & Social Influence, 2020)
- In England, 64% of volunteers participated in volunteer activities at least once in the previous year. In the meantime, 39% stated they participated at least once a month. (2020, Gov.uk).
- In terms of volunteers' gender, females made up 66 percent of the population in England who took part in

voluntary activities in 2020. Meanwhile, 61 percent of the participants were men. (2020, Government of the United Kingdom)

- Seventy percent of volunteers in England were between the ages of 65 and 74.Meanwhile, 67% of those polled was between the ages of 35 and 49. (2020, Government of the United Kingdom)

Donor Demographics and Behavior

It's no surprise that the majority of donors to NGOs in the United States and the United Kingdom are older citizens who have had the opportunity to develop their fortune over time. This isn't to say that young people aren't helping out where they can. It's also worth noting that female donors outnumber male donors in the United Kingdom.

- In the United States, the average donor is 64 years old. (2020, Blackbaud)
- Non-cash assets are more likely to be given by 27% of contributors. (2020, Freewill)
- In 2020, overall donations grew by 2%. Online donations, on the other hand, are expected to climb by 21% in 2020. (2020, Blackbaud)
- According to a poll, charitable organizations had a 25% retention rate for first-time, online-only donors. Multi-year, online-only donors, on the other hand, had a retention rate of 66 percent.(2020, Blackbaud)
- The quantity of money donated will not alter as a result of the COVID-19 epidemic, according to 54% of donors. On the other hand, 25% stated they would increase their donations. (2020, Fidelity Charitable)

- During the epidemic, 43% of donors stated that they intended to continue donating to the charity that they support. On the other hand, 21% said they don't know or haven't considered it, while 16% indicated they are helping new NGOs. (2020, Fidelity Charitable)
- During the epidemic, 24% of young Americans stated they had donated products and/or services to help others. (Cause & Social Influence, 2020)
- In England, 75% of the population donated to charity in 2020. During the same year, 79% of ladies donated to charity, while 70% of males did so. (2020, Government of the United Kingdom)
- By 2020, 85 percent of those aged 75 and up in England will have donated to charity. Only 55% of people between the ages of 16 and 24 did the same. (2020, Government of the United Kingdom)

COVID-19's Impact on Nonprofits

The COVID-19 epidemic has had severe repercussions across all industries, and the nonprofit sector is no exception. Donations and earned income fell for a large percentage of NGOs in the United States. Furthermore, stricter health and safety regulations necessitate increased costs for NGOs. Nonprofits have restructured their programs to address COVID-related issues.

- Due to the pandemic, 90 percent of organizations in Nevada reported a decrease in individual donations. (Project for Nonprofit Education Survey, 2021)
- In West Virginia, 90 percent of organizations faced event cancellations, resulting in revenue loss. (Project for Nonprofit Education Survey, 2021)

- In Texas, 68.3 percent of non-profit organizations reported a decrease in revenue from service fees or membership dues.(Project for Nonprofit Education Survey, 2021)
- Because of the pandemic, 34.7 percent of NGOs in Texas and 20.3 percent of nonprofits in Alabama and Georgia reported delays in grant processing. (Project for Nonprofit Education Survey, 2021)
- Additional COVID-19-related expenses, such as cleaning protocols and personal protective equipment, were reported by 57.8% of Connecticut charities. (Project for Nonprofit Education Survey, 2021)
- Because of the COVID-19 pandemic, 40.1 percent of non-governmental organizations (NGOs) in Texas have reduced their working hours.(Project for Nonprofit Education Survey, 2021)
- In reaction to COVID-19, 53% of organizations in the United States and abroad have launched special appeals or emergency funds. (2020 CCS Fundraising).
- With a special focus on COVID-19 initiatives, 32% of charitable organizations in the US and abroad have changed or expanded their cases. (2020 CCS Fundraising).
- The pandemic has had a substantial impact on 51 percent of NGOs' fundraising and development, as well as volunteer services programs. The epidemic has also had a substantial impact on the delivery of programs and services, according to 55% of respondents. (2020, Fidelity Charitable)

Providing Advocacy in the Face of Adversity

Nonprofit data reveals that these groups may generate billions of dollars in revenue, primarily through public donations. People demonstrate their support for organizations by making donations or offering their time and effort to help them.

Working for a nonprofit during a pandemic entails dealing with delayed funds, lower donations, reduced work hours, and other challenges. Nonprofits, on the other hand, have risen to the situation by adapting their programs to include COVID-19 problems. These organizations can rise above hardship and continue to carry out their purpose with such flexibility, along with a love for their cause and the correct nonprofit collaboration software.

BryteBridge President Brian Davis stated, "Nonprofits and the services they provide are important to a flourishing society." "This research can help new organizations overcome difficulties so they can better serve their constituents by shedding light on frequent challenges they confront."

The following are some of the report's key takeaways on the pandemic's impact:

- About 79 percent of NGOs say the pandemic has resulted in a drop in revenue. These revenue decreases were stated to be 50% or greater by 38% of respondents.
- Only 25% of NGOs stated they had enough cash flow to pay expenses comfortably without making any budget cuts.

- To survive the epidemic, about 60% of NGOs had to employ furloughs.

The following are some of the report's key takeaways on new NGOs' main concerns:

Compliance problems and fundraising are the top two challenges that charity under the age of five encounters.

1. For 37% of NGOs, fundraising will be their primary issue in the future.
2. The first year's priorities include obtaining 501(c)(3) certification and developing fundraising strategies.
3. In their first year, 73% of organizations require assistance with volunteer management.

The Nonprofit Sector and the Pandemic

The pandemic has destroyed numerous industries, including the nonprofit sector.

According to a recent analysis by Candid, previously the Foundation Center and GuideStar, up to one-third of US NGOs are in danger of closing as a result of the COVID-19 pandemic's financial impact.

Most nonprofits are well-positioned to weather a brief economic downturn, but not a big economic disaster. As we watch the economic downturn caused by the epidemic unfold, it's vital to realize that many nonprofit organizations are at risk of closure.

The study looked at how approximately 300,000 organizations would do in 20 distinct economic scenarios, ranging from the baseline of no crisis to a severe economic recession, with the worst-case scenario projecting the closure of 38 percent of nonprofits throughout the country. Even the less bleak scenarios resulted in double-digit closures. The study's findings were particularly worrisome since they highlighted the impact on Black, Indigenous, and People of Color (BIPOC)-led groups, increasing the gaps in philanthropy that already exist in our society.

The following are some of the study's findings:

- Candid tracked more than $20 billion in funding for COVID-19 in 2020 across the globe, with companies paying for 44% of the total.
- Arts and entertainment-related non-profits are the most vulnerable, as they rely on ticket sales (which are almost non-existent during a pandemic), have little cash on hand, and are unable to cut costs.
- Over the period, nearly a quarter of all donations tracked by Candid for all organizations were allocated for specific recipients in BIPOC groups.
- 23% of donations were made specifically for BIPOC communities or organizations that serve them.
- When high-net-worth individuals were eliminated from the mix (leaving just donations from companies, foundations, and public charities), the percentage directed to communities of color fell to 13%, putting BIPOC-led groups at risk.

Where does this leave the nonprofit industry?

This difficult environment pushes organizations to consider how they can survive as gifts get fewer and resources become scarce.

Many NGOs will undoubtedly try to save costs by narrowing their focus, cutting services, or reducing staff. Some nonprofits may desire to be a part of a merger or purchase to increase capacity or profitability, but this will result in fewer NGOs surviving. This is especially disappointing because the nonprofit sector had shown evidence of resiliency prior to the pandemic.

How Do Nonprofit Organizations Make Money?

Nonprofits must raise funds in order to carry out their altruistic goals. To raise the funds needed to run the business and pay your salary, you can seek grants and hold fundraisers. Renting property, selling donated products, and making investments are all options for your organization to generate revenue. However, if your nonprofit earns money in ways that are unrelated to its objective, that revenue will be taxable. If your nonprofit is set up to provide food to the homeless but raises revenue by purchasing and selling secondhand cars, the IRS will almost certainly deem those contributions taxable.

Even a non-profit organization requires funding to maintain its daily activities. Nonprofits can use an income stream to fund day-to-day operations by paying for office space, materials, and staff. The funds raised can also be used to cover travel and media expenses, which will help get the word out about what you're doing.

The manner in which charities generate funds has a significant impact on whether any profits they make are taxable. If the money originates from things connected to the nonprofit's activities, it's usually deemed nontaxable profits. Related profits include donations, ticket sales from charitable events, and item sales to raise funds for group programs.

Unrelated activities, on the other hand, can be tax-free as long as taxes are charged. Unrelated behaviors include selling unclaimed door prizes at an event and keeping the cash. While unrelated activities are allowed, unrelated activity income must be kept to a minimum to prevent losing the nonprofit's 501(c)(3) registration.

Nonprofit Fundraising Options

Individual donations, which accounted for 70% of all gifts in 2017, are one of the most prevalent ways for NGOs to raise funds. Foundations, corporations, and private bequests are all important financing sources. As a result, a considerable portion of the time will be spent courting public support.

However, the organization's technique for raising funds is extremely dependent on the nonprofit itself. Girl Scouts sell cookies every year, but troops can also come up with their own revenue-generating ideas, such as publishing cookbooks, making crafts for local fairs, or organizing walkathons. Many NGOs collect money by holding special events like dinners where influential members of the community pay top dollar for a seat at the table.

Salaries for Non-Profit Organizations

You should look into alternative choices if you're searching for a job that will allow you to live a life of luxury. Nonprofit jobs are ideal for folks who wish to make a difference with their efforts. Because charities are more concerned with promoting a cause than with generating a profit, wages are maintained as cheap as possible in order to attract talent. Nonprofit jobs are ideal for folks who wish to make a difference with their efforts.

According to standard nonprofit salaries, an executive director's salary, for example, averages $50,000 per year. In all industries, the average income for an executive director is $77,000, which is $22,000 higher than the national average. Half of the time, charities would hire a limited number of people to undertake higher-level duties, with unpaid volunteers filling in the gaps. For example, the average salary for a volunteer administrator is $38,000. Working for a cause you care about, on the other hand, may be worth a reduced salary.

Nonprofits and Ethics

Let's face it: the nonprofit's programs require financial support. It's vital, though, that you keep rigorous ethical standards in mind when you come up with revenue-generating concepts. A statement of principles can help you define standards for what your organization will and will not do to increase income.

Ethics, on the other hand, goes beyond misappropriating money. Money that has been polluted might be an issue as well. If a potential source of income benefits your firm but goes against its core ideals, declining the money may be the best option. If your salary with a nonprofit is exorbitant, you may face criticism from the public and volunteers, as well as dealing with your own personal ethical difficulties.

Resources

Grants.gov

If you're based in the United States, the US government has a searchable online database of government grants to help you find what you need. Click on "Find Grant Opportunities" on the left side of the page, then select "Basic Search" to search using a keyword or a combination of keywords to find the right federal grants for your work.

Pro tip: Join the Grants.gov mailing list to receive a daily or weekly digest of current federal funding opportunities.

Foundation Center

Foundation Center is particularly useful for its extensive directory and free resources. This is the primary online source for grants available through private foundations, corporate foundations, and other nonprofits that accept grant proposals.

Google Ad Grants

Google Ad Grants program offers $10,000 USD of in-kind advertising every month from Google Ads, an online advertising solution from Google.

Grantwatch.com

Their search engine identifies grants for universities, hospitals, government agencies, schools, community-based organizations, faith-based organizations, research institutions, and some small businesses and individuals.

Guidestar

Guidestar provides information on all kinds of nonprofits, including foundations. You can register for free and use the advanced search capabilities to find the 990-PFs of foundations.

Local/State Funding

Depending on where you're based, it might be useful to try finding grants at a municipal or state level. Contact the relevant local or state departments and/or look through their websites. You might want to consider contacting the Department of Health, Jobs and Family Services, Human Services, Department of Development, Small Business Development, Department of Education, Department of Transportation, or City Councils. Ask about the grants they have available.

Board members

An often underutilized resource, your Board is a potential grant goldmine. As you do your research for funders, take note of foundation trustees and staff and forward those names to your board to see if there are any connections.

Go outside the box

Look at annual reports and newspaper articles. Who is giving to organizations that are similar to yours? Put any like-minded funder on your mailing list and start sending those materials about your organization.

Global Funding Opportunities for Individuals, Small Businesses, and Nonprofits

GrantStation—updating a comprehensive list of organizations providing COVID-19 emergency assistance for nonprofits, individuals, and small businesses all over the globe

Candid.—Compiling a list of more than 200 emergency financial resources broken down geographically for individuals, nonprofits, and small businesses

Global Entrepreneurship Network —sharing a hub for international support of entrepreneurs sorted by country and resource type provided

United Way —committing to supporting individuals and communities worldwide who are impacted by the COVID-19 outbreak through hardship assistance

International Women's Media Foundation —Accepting applications for grants up to $2,000 for women who identify journalists facing significant financial hardship, lost work, were recently laid off or who urgently need assistance due to the effect of COVID-19

Women's Business Enterprise National Council (WBENC) —sharing a robust list of grants and financial resources for small businesses, globally, some specifically supporting women-led businesses

Council on Foundations—curating a list of self-reported funders globally who are actively providing financial support to nonprofit organizations

Skoll Foundation—providing a list of global funders and COVID-19 resources for community organizations

Worldwide Initiatives for Grantmaker Support (WINGS)— compiling a global list and providing a map of funders and resources supporting individual and nonprofits globally

Also take a look at:

The Grantsmanship Center

Community Foundation Locator

The Chronicle of Philanthropy

GrantStation

Instrumentl

Mozilla.org

Philanthropic-Programs

https://knightfoundation.org/apply

CNE

Nonprofit Expert

The Stable Company

Fundraiser Help

Grantsplus Grants Opportunities

Chapter Three - Nonprofit Organization Location

Brick and Mortar VS Online Nonprofit Organizations

Online nonprofit organizations are fantastic, but there are numerous reasons to prefer a brick-and-mortar nonprofit organization.

The internet has irrevocably altered our shopping habits. Many individuals use the internet to shop for clothing, groceries, and anything else they want or need. Is it, however, always the best option to go online? Though internet nonprofit organizations are convenient, there are many compelling reasons to visit a physical nonprofit organization.

If you're thinking about starting a nonprofit organization, you should think about it thoroughly. When selecting whether to go online or offline, there are a few things to consider.

Humans have a long history of bartering and trading goods in exchange for one another. While the fundamentals have stayed constant throughout history – you give something in order to receive something – the mechanisms have changed over time. People have continued to engage in nonprofit organizations in the hope of profit and success, from the agora of Ancient Greece to the modern supermarket, and from high-end boutiques to internet retailers.

If one were to divide today's nonprofit organization methods into two groups, they would be:

1. Brick and Mortar nonprofit organizations, and
2. Online nonprofit organizations

The Brick and Mortar Nonprofit

The traditional form of doing Nonprofit- brick and mortar - may be quite costly and time consuming to set up. If the firm is to have any chance of flourishing, it is critical to secure a suitable site, and such valued properties are not cheap. Then there's the overhead, which includes things like taxes, utility expenses, inventory, and labor.

The Benefits:

- Perhaps the most significant advantage of a physical nonprofit organization over an online nonprofit organization is that it allows customers to physically touch, feel, and scrutinize a product or service before making a purchase choice.

- Scams abound on the internet, and many have taken advantage of these chances. As a result, a brick and mortar nonprofit organization may provide clients with peace of mind, a sense of trust, and dependability.

- Find the perfect location, preferably in a high-traffic area, and people may just walk into your nonprofit organization—and become customers - without ever having heard of your marketing initiatives.

The Negatives:

- As previously stated, the launch and overhead costs of a brick and mortar nonprofit organization are typically rather high.

- Once you've posted the 'Closed' sign, your shop is officially closed till the next day.

Online Nonprofit Firm

It is relatively easy to set up a more current, graphic style of doing nonprofit. You'll still have to do a lot of the same things, including market research and promotional efforts, but the beginning and overhead expenditures will be far lower.

The Benefits:

- An internet store may and does stay open and ready for business 24 hours a day, seven days a week, 365 days a year.

- If you've managed to make the proper amount of noise in the correct areas, you'll be able to attract more customers to your small business than you could with a traditional nonprofit organization.

- There are no space restrictions and no sales representatives are required. If 50 consumers go into a brick and mortar location, you'll most likely run out of both. With an internet nonprofit organization, you may serve thousands of people at once.

The Negatives:

- The major disadvantage of an internet **Nonprofit**, in comparison to a physical Nonprofit, is that there is very little, if any, interaction with customers.

- Because you won't be confined by shelf space to showcase things in an internet Nonprofit, it's surprisingly easy to get distracted. It is critical that you choose a specialization for your nonprofit organization and stick to it.

Each of these options, both conventional and modern, has its own set of benefits and drawbacks. And, while you can argue about which one is superior till the end of time, they are both here to stay for the foreseeable future. If you can afford it, opening a physical as well as an online for your Nonprofit Organization is the best approach to being successful.

So, what kind of nonprofit organizations do you run? Regardless of which option you choose, you must execute your marketing strategy correctly. You'll still need to attend numerous networking events and generate leads for your company. The strategies remain the same, but the tactics change on a regular basis. To cultivate loyal customers, make sure you're using one of the finest CRM systems, such as Leads Helper, to build a leads database and send targeted track able marketing messages to your audience.

Internet Nonprofit Organizations vs. Traditional Nonprofit Organizations

I used to consider creating and operating a number of trading and consulting Nonprofit Organization, but after learning more about the benefits of internet Nonprofit Organization, my ideas for making significant money in the future have shifted. I believe that once people learn about the internet's commercial miracles, they will experience a paradigm change that will render brick and store enterprises obsolete.

In comparison to a traditional brick and mortar Nonprofit Organizations, starting an online nonprofit organization does not necessitate a large amount of capital. Forget about the high costs of commercial space leasing, furniture, and personnel that traditional brick-and-mortar nonprofit organizations necessitate. Working capital for an online nonprofit is as simple as a PC with an internet connection. Consider how much money can be saved simply by making that distinction. Why not lower the expense of running the business to two or three figures instead of four to five, or even six? Unless further advertising costs are included, the cost of running an internet business will never be less than three figures.

In terms of Return on Assets, the profit created by an internet nonprofit is always higher than that of a brick and mortar nonprofit organization. Similarly, internet nonprofit organization owners will always make more money than brick and mortar nonprofit organization owners. The reason for this is because brick and mortar nonprofit organization owners invest a significant amount of money to establish and manage their company in a specific location. Internet nonprofit organizations, on the other hand, spend significantly less on startup and operational costs. What makes online businesses so profitable is their capacity to reach millions of clients globally via the internet, but brick-and-mortar nonprofit organizations an only reach and profit from customers in their immediate vicinity.

The Internet and brick-and-mortar Nonprofit Organizations function and are regulated in distinct ways. Internet Nonprofit Organizations operate in a virtual marketplace and can be monitored from anywhere with an internet connection, whereas brick and mortar Nonprofit Organizations are limited to a single physical location. What's noteworthy about online Nonprofit Organizations is that their owners may operate and oversee their firms from the comfort of their own homes or while on vacation, something that brick and mortar Nonprofit Organizations owners cannot do.

As an internet Nonprofit Organizations, life would undoubtedly be a dream comes true because they are the only ones who can work from home or travel while making money, unlike brick and mortar Nonprofit Organizations who are forever stuck in the same location and struggle to keep operating costs low in order to keep the business afloat.

Resources

<u>eFulfillment Service</u> - This service is inexpensive and interfaces with the marketplaces you may already be using (Etsy, eBay, etc).

<u>Rakuten Super Logistics</u> — as part of a larger corporation, Rakuten is able to provide value-added services that fulfillment-only businesses cannot.

<u>Fulfillment.com</u> is a service that caters to businesses that sell globally.

<u>CensusViewer</u> is a free program that lets you view U.S. Census data visually on a map or in data reports for cities, counties, and entire states.

<u>Google Trends</u>: Use Google Trends to see what people are looking for and how the volume of searches for significant topics has changed over time.

Look no farther than <u>LivePlan</u> if you need to design a business plan, create a budget, or anticipate your sales and cash flow.

<u>Zoho One</u> is an all-in-one operating system that keeps track of all aspects of a company's operations.

<u>Asana</u> - A work and project management platform that offers a 50% discount for all nonprofits that qualify, which will assist your employees in keeping track of their to-do list and projects.

<u>Zapier</u> - Big workload that can use some automation? Zapier offers a 15% discount on thousands of automation "triggers"

that integrate with most of the apps and programs you use on a daily basis and many listed above.

Slack - Communicate effectively with your team with an 85% discount, with a free plan for organizations with fewer than 250 employees.

Animoto :: animoto.com

Animoto is an online video maker that makes it easy for anyone to drag and drop their way to powerful and professional marketing videos.

CauseVid: causevid.com

CauseVid allows users to easily create personalized Thank You videos that can be delivered by email. See also **ThankView**.

ClipChamp :: clipchamp.com

ClimpChamp is a video editing tool that empowers users to easily create video ads for Facebook and Instagram.

Lumen5 :: lumen5.com

Lumen5 converts articles and blog posts into video content – ideal for social media.

Veed.io :: veed.io

Veed.io is an easy-to-use video editing tool that easily allows you to add subtitles and photos and graphics to videos. See also **Kapwing** and **WeVideo**.

Dropbox :: *dropbox.com*

Dropbox is a cloud storage service (sometimes referred to as an online backup service) that is frequently used for file sharing and collaboration.

Dulingo :: *duolingo.com*

Dulingo provides access to free online language learning tools. For nonprofit social media managers that work internationally, Dulingo's design and gamification make it fun to learn the basics of a new language.

Chapter Four - Nonprofit Name Selection

Many Nonprofit organizations are still named after their proprietors if you drive through any rural community. In some places, names like "Walker's Drugstore" and "Carl's Café" are still prominent, although naming your business after yourself isn't always the greatest option. Many rural American towns are stuck in time, part of a micro-economy with little room for expansion and, in many cases, on the decline. Most aspiring nonprofit owners do not intend to launch a company in this manner; hence most Nonprofit organization should avoid naming their company after themselves.

There are a few instances where employing your own name is the most effective marketing strategy. Use your own name if you are a well-known specialist in your sector and buyers will be compelled to buy your product or service because of your name. For obvious reasons, artists such as clothing designers and painters use their own names, and clients have grown to recognize styles by the artists' names. Small construction companies are sometimes named after their founders, while most national and international startups are moving away from this practice. Doctors, lawyers, and accountants form businesses under their own names, but they rely on their good reputation to generate business. Consider finding a more detailed approach to identifying your endeavor if your Nonprofit organization idea does not rely on your current reputation to thrive.

One disadvantage of utilizing your name as a nonprofit name is that it provides no information to potential clients about what you do. Anything from pencil top erasers to luxury yachts could be sold by "Smith, Inc." Even "Smith's Boats" isn't going to help you stand out from the crowd. Anything from small models to ocean liners might be sold by the company. Rivercraft boats, on the other hand, conjure up images of mid-sized, well-built boats intended for usage on rivers.

Choosing the proper name for your nonprofit company is no longer as simple as it once was. Even 20 years ago, any name you liked could definitely be used, even if it was already taken by another company in a different field. Your alternatives have become much more constrained since the emergence of the internet. Every new nonprofit organization requires an internet presence, and having a domain name that matches your nonprofit name is the best chance. Finding a nonprofit organization you like that is also available online is getting harder with over 100 million domain names currently in use.

Step 1: Developing A Nonprofit Organization Name

So you've made your choice. You've come up with a brilliant concept. You're ready to start a nonprofit organization and pursue your passion. You're just one step away from starting your own nonprofit firm. You're one step closer to being your own boss. You're one step closer to becoming a nonprofit owner, but you still need to come up with a nonprofit organization name...

A nonprofit organization name is something that should never be taken lightly.

When choosing a name for your nonprofit, there are numerous factors to consider. Is the nonprofit local, national, or international, depending on what you want to do, where you want to do business, and what industry you want to get into? Is your nonprofit company involved in the construction, manufacture, sale, purchase, trade, or distribution of something? Each of these criteria can have an impact on the name you choose. Is your nonprofit company a non-profit? Is your nonprofit company a member of a group? Is it a family-owned company?

I'd like you to acquire a piece of paper and a pen before I start going over some examples. Make a list of several names that would be appropriate for your company. Keep all of the names close together so you can compare them and go through them again and again.

Let's have a look at some of the samples that are impacted by the following statements:

Using your first and last names:

Real Estate is a service-based business (Ex. Lemieux Realtor) - Mortgage Consultant (The Lemieux Mortgage Group) - Legal Services (Lemieux Law Firm) - Martin's Design Concepts (design) - Composition (Lemieux Writing Services) - Business (Lemieux Enterprises) - Independent contractors (Lemieux Building Group) - Martin's Reno Services (renovators) - Printing services (Lemieux Print Shop)

Based on a product: - Pizza Joint (Martin's Pizza Delight) - Toys (Martin's Toy Shop) - Clothing (Lemieux Fashion) - Home equipment (Lemieux Appliances)

As you can see, all of these business name choices refer to two things: my name and what I do. The objective is to include your personal name and industry into your nonprofit name. It doesn't matter if you use your first or last name.

What is important is that you like your given name. A nonprofit name can live with you until you die, and it has the ability to be passed down through your family for generations.

Names with a twist:

These illustrations will be something I came up with on the spur of the moment to offer you some inspiration. Each name will be accompanied by a phrase that will explain what the name means.

Based on a service: - Online Promotion ("eMarket Promo" - Internet Marketing Promotion for Your nonprofit) - Art Direction ("Crystal Graphics Firm" - Graphics that wow people) Clean Cut Barbers ("Clean Cut Barbers" - Haircuts that clean up your style) - Networking for Business ("NETeGroup" - Entrepreneurs Grouping For More Business Leads)

Hydraulic systems are based on a product ("ProHyd Systems" - Professional hydraulics that last). - Cues for the pool ("StickBall Cues" - A pool cue that sticks to its game) - Energy Bars ("SafeBars" - A power bar safe for the whole family)

A simple play on words, combined with brief descriptions of your product or service, can help you come up with something a little more original. Despite the fact that these names were produced in less than 10 minutes, take your time with them; you should never rush these things. A business name should never occur to you in a flash. Allow some time for the thoughts to develop. Even if you think you've found the perfect name, leave it alone and revisit it frequently. Inquire about your selections with friends, family, and coworkers.

Names of local businesses:

Locally based services should have a name that explains what they do. It should be straightforward and memorable. To illustrate what I mean, I'll use my own location (Hamilton, Ontario) in these cases.

- Lawn Care Across the City (Hamilton Lawn Care) - Real Estate - Mortgage Brokers (Hamilton Mortgage Group) (Greater-Hamilton Homes) - Job placement service (Hamilton Employers)

- Insurance Brokers - Insurance (Ontario Insurance Specialists) - Delivery of parcels (Ontario Mailing Systems) - Apple Farm (Ontario Apple Trees) - Movers (Relocators of Ontario)

- Baby Clothes - Baby (Canadian Baby Wear) - Personal computers (Computers Made in Canada) - Professional advisors (Canadian Consulting Group) - Printing services (PrintCanada)

For suggestions, it's a little easier to come up with a nonprofit name that targets your local area. Always make an effort to include your city, province/state, or country in the equation when describing the service region you provide. Make sure to look for other nonprofit with the same name on the internet. Because of how easy it can be for people to remember your name, many local nonprofits choose this way of selecting a wonderful name.

This finishes my suggestions for coming up with a nonprofit name. I still have a lot to teach you about naming, but it would take me to write a novel, and I want to cover all of the essentials in this tutorial, not just one.

Step 2: Search for Duplicate Names

Once you've narrowed down your nonprofit name list to 1-5 options, it's time to perform some web research to see if anyone else has already stolen your name.

Everyone's online search experience will be unique. Depending on the type of nonprofit you wish to start, there are several approaches to look for duplicate nonprofit names.

When conducting an internet search, you must first determine:

1) Are you a local, provincial/state-wide, national, or worldwide nonprofit?

2) Will you register your name as a trademark or copyright? Also...

A) Are there any other nonprofit companies with the same name as you?

B) Does one of your competitors own a trademark or copyright to a name that sounds similar to yours?

1.1) Geographical:

This is the one that is most likely to be found. You may usually run a search within Google/Yahoo/MSN with your business name in quotes, such as "My Term" in "My City", "Province/State", "Country" (for example, search for "Lawn Care Guys in Hamilton, Ontario, Canada") to check if exact results for that name are found. To achieve different results, try the same thing without the quotations. If you do obtain results, look through the website to discover if the results were "manufactured" by search engines for their own purposes, or if they are a true nonprofit name.

Don't forget to check the results to see if they match the type of nonprofit you want to start.

The industry in which you want to work has an impact on the availability of your name. For instance, you may call your company "Hamilton Lawn Maintenance." I promise that when you make a search, search engines will mix the words "Hamilton" and "Lawn" and "Maintenance" to construct their results. I'm sure there's a lawn maintenance service in Hamilton. Can you see how that might muddle your search results? Don't get disappointed if you find several matches while searching online; this is just the beginning.

1.2) Statewide / Provincial:

You'll want to search in the same way you did in "1.1) Local," but now you'll want to eliminate the "City" from your searches to see if you can locate a name that sounds similar to yours right away. If you get any results from your search, look into it further by visiting the website (s) you found.

If a possible competitor already has the name you desire, scratch it and forget about it. You don't want to end up in court later for something that may be avoided today.

1.3) National:

Same thing, but in your searches, only add your "Country."

1.4) International:

Simply look for your company name in "Quotes." Instead of using a country-specific search engine like Google.ca, conduct your queries on Google.com. Search engines will be able to provide you an accurate match for your business name if you include quotes. It won't matter if other companies use your name unless you're directly associated in the same industry and they possess the copyright to that name.

1.5) Copyright / Trademark:

"A trademark or trade mark is a distinctive symbol of some type that is used by an individual, business organization, or other legal entity to distinguish its products and/or services from those of other entities and to uniquely identify the source of its products and/or services to consumers." Wikipedia

When looking for a nonprofit organization name online, avoid names that are similar to a trademark. If you copy a trademark, you could face serious consequences, including a lawsuit. In fact, a gentleman on the internet has been debating this concept for quite some time. Nissan, a well-known automobile manufacturer, owns a trademark on its name and logo, but not on http://www.Nissan.com . They missed the deadline to purchase the domain name, and they are now suing the owner for ten million dollars in damages, a lawsuit that has been ongoing since 1999.

If you want to trademark your name, you must first ensure that no one else is using it. Phrases, words, logos, and images all fall within this category. The difficult aspect is rebranding an existing product. For example, you would have a lot of trouble trademarking "Business Name" in Canada because so many individuals already use the phrases "business name" and "business name" together online before you ever filed a trademark application.

I advise you to employ an expert to assist you with your trade marking requirements. This will provide you access to government databases that will allow you to browse through past trademarks and assist you in searching for other names that may prevent you from trademarking your name.

For some, trademarking is prohibitively expensive, but once you have one, no one else can use your good name for anything else without your express written consent. This was a mistake I made with my first company, "Smartadz." People began to use smartadz for their own objectives over time, some for good and some for harm.

Step 3: Checking a Government Database for Trademarks

For the most part, you can conduct a nonprofit organization name search at your local nonprofit organization name register office.

Resources

Domain Name Generator - This clever application searches for the right domain name using synonyms, suffixes, prefixes, and more.

WordLab name generators - For you to consider, this keyword/sentence generator generates fully random choices.

Namelix - This website generates short, brand able names based on keywords you provide.

BNG - Business Name Generator generates millions of results based on your search queries.

Namesmith.io is a website where you can create a unique name. Namesmith.io is a more creative tool that includes both random and curated alternatives.

<u>Wordoid</u> - Users enter keywords on the left and are given names that start with, terminate with, or contain a fragment of the original inquiry.

BrainyQuote :: <u>brainyquote.com</u>

BrainyQuote is a directory of inspirational quotes — ideal for creating social media graphics.

SlideShare :: <u>slideshare.net</u>

SlideShare is the largest presentation-sharing website in the world. It's a great online home for decks from speaking engagements and presentations about your organization's work.

VolunteerMatch :: <u>volunteermatch.org</u>

VolunteerMatch is an online portal to volunteer opportunities posted by over 100K nonprofits.

SenderScore - How it works: Planning to send fundraising emails from your organization's email account? Make sure that your domain has a good reputation and that you're not getting into spam folders by checking your SenderScore and looking for ways to improve your email deliverability.

<u>LinkedIn</u> -Find volunteers, employees, and so much more with a LinkedIn nonprofit account. Discounts are available upon request for nonprofits at <u>sales@linkedin.com</u>.

<u>BuzzSumo</u> - Analyze what content works best with your demographic, or what's working best for similar organizations to optimize your marketing campaigns. For discounted pricing for nonprofits, email <u>help@buzzsumo.com</u>.

SurveyMonkey :: surveymonkey.com

SurveyMonkey is an online survey service ideal for gathering feedback from donors and supporters. For multilingual surveys, see **Alchemer**.

Year.ly :: yearly.report

Yearly makes it easy to design annual reports, event recaps, donor proposals, and board presentations.

Calendly :: calendly.com

Calendly enables users to select time slots via email to easily schedule meetings through Google, Outlook, Office 365, or iCloud calendar.

To search for domain names, simply go to:

http://www.GoDaddy.com
https://www.namecheap.com

Chapter Five - Nonprofit Organization Essentials

Starting a nonprofit organization necessitates perseverance, motivation, and knowledge. So you've got some great ideas and a strong staff to help you make them a reality. Your modest startup nonprofit organization is unquestionably on its way to creating an impression.

However, you'll need a solid arsenal to achieve your objectives. You'll need gear and essentials to get the work done and move your startup forward in the direction you want it to go.

With that in mind, no matter what area of nonprofit organization you're in, there are vital cornerstones that no nonprofit organization in today's world can thrive without:

How to Pick the Right Legal Structure for Your Nonprofit Organization

Choosing the appropriate legal structure is an important aspect of running a nonprofit company. It's critical to understand your alternatives, whether you're just starting out or your nonprofit company is expanding.

Depending on the entity's finance and liability structure, partnerships can operate as either a sole proprietorship or a limited liability partnership.

If it cannot be established that members of an LLC engaged in an illegal, unethical, or negligent manner in carrying out the business's activities, they are immune from personal accountability for the debts of the company.

Corporations can sell stock to raise money for expansion, but sole proprietors can only get money from their personal bank accounts, personal credit, or taking on partners.

This paper is for nonprofit organization owners who want to learn more about the various legal structures for nonprofit organizations.

Analyzing your nonprofit organization's goals and examining local, state, and federal laws are the first steps in determining the best legal structure for your company. You can choose the legal structure that best suits your nonprofit company's culture by establishing your aims. You can adjust your legal form as your company expands to meet its new needs.

To assist you in deciding on the right legal structure for your nonprofit organization company, we've developed a list of the most popular forms of nonprofit entities and their distinguishing characteristics.

Different kinds of nonprofit arrangements

Sole proprietorships, partnerships, limited liability companies, corporations, and cooperatives are the most frequent types of business entities. Here's more information on each legal framework.

1. Sole proprietorship

This is the most basic type of nonprofit structure. In a sole proprietorship, one person is solely liable for the profits and obligations of the organization.

"A sole proprietorship allows you to be your own boss and manage a nonprofit organization from home without having to have a physical storefront," said Deborah Sweeney, CEO of MyCorporation. "This company does not provide for the separation or protection of personal and professional assets, which could become a problem as your firm expands and more components of it hold you responsible."

The cost of a proprietorship varies depending on the market in which your company operates. State and federal fees, taxes, equipment demands, office space, banking costs, and any professional services your business decides to contract are all examples of early expenses. Freelance writers, tutors, bookkeepers, cleaning service providers, and babysitters are examples of these enterprises.

Some of the advantages of this business structure are as follows:

Setup is simple. The simplest legal structure to establish is a sole proprietorship. This may be the best form for you if your nonprofit organization company is solely owned by you. Because you have no partners or executive boards to answer to, there is relatively little paperwork.

The price is low. License fees and firm taxes are the only fees involved with a proprietorship, and they vary based on which state you live in.

Deduction for taxes. You may be qualified for certain company tax deductions, such as a health insurance deduction, because you and your nonprofit organization are a single entity.

Exit is simple. Creating a sole proprietorship is simple, as is quitting one. You can disband your firm at any time as a sole proprietor with no official paperwork necessary. For example, if you open a daycare center and decide to close it down, you can simply stop operating it and advertise your services.

Examples of sole proprietorships: One of the most prevalent legal structures for nonprofit organizations is the sole proprietorship. Many well-known nonprofit organizations began as sole proprietorships and developed into multibillion-dollar firms.

Here are a few examples:

- eBay
- JC Penny
- Walmart
- Marriott Hotels

2. Partnership

This firm is owned by two or more people. A general partnership, in which all profits are shared equally, and a limited partnership, in which only one partner controls the company while the other person (or persons) contributes to and receives a portion of the profits, are the two varieties. Depending on the entity's finance and liability structure, partnerships can operate as either a sole proprietorship or a limited liability partnership (LLP).

"This entity is great for anyone who wants to start a company with a family member, friend, or business partner, such as a restaurant or an agency," Sweeney added. "Within the corporate structure, a partnership allows participants to share earnings and losses and make decisions jointly. Keep in mind that you will be held liable for your judgments as well as your company partner's behavior."

A general partnership can be more expensive than a sole proprietorship because you'll need an attorney to analyze your partnership agreement. The price range is influenced by the attorney's experience and region. For a general partnership to be effective, it must be a win-win situation for both parties.

Google is an example of this type of company. Larry Page and Sergey Brin co-founded Google in 1995 and grew it from a modest search engine to the world's most popular search engine. The co-founders met while earning their doctorates at Stanford University and later left to build a beta version of their search engine. They obtained $1 million in cash from investors shortly after, and Google began seeing thousands of visits every day. They have a combined net worth of nearly $46 billion as a result of their ownership of 16% of Google.

Here are a few of the benefits of forming a firm partnership:

It's simple to make. There isn't as much paperwork to file as there is with a single proprietorship. If your state requires you to conduct company under a false name ("doing business as," or DBA), you'll need to obtain a Certificate of Conducting Business as Partners and write an Articles of Partnership agreement, both of which come with additional expenses. In most cases, a firm license is also required.

Possibility of expansion. When there are multiple owners, you have a better chance of getting a company loan. If you have a bad credit score, bankers may consider two credit lines rather than one.

Taxation with a difference. General partnerships are required to file federal tax Form 1065 as well as state forms, but they rarely pay income tax. On their individual income tax forms, both partners disclose their joint income or loss. You and your friend are co-owners if you founded a bakery with a friend and organized the business as a general partnership. Each owner brings to the company a particular amount of knowledge and working capital, which might influence each partner's share of the company and contribution. Let's say you contributed the most seed capital to the company; it's possible that you'll be given a bigger share percentage, thereby making you the majority owner.

Examples of partnerships

Partnerships are one of the most frequent types of firm formations, second only to sole proprietorships. Here are some examples of successful collaborations:

- Warner Brothers
- Hewlett Packard
- Microsoft
- Apple
- Ben & Jerry's
- Twitter

3. Limited Liability Corporation (LLC)

A limited liability corporation (LLC) is a hybrid entity that allows owners, partners, or shareholders to reduce their personal obligations while still reaping the tax and flexibility benefits of a partnership. If it cannot be established that members of an LLC engaged in an illegal, unethical, or negligent manner in carrying out the business's activities, they are shielded from personal accountability for the debts of the company.

"Limited liability companies were created to give business owners the liability protection that corporations have while allowing gains and losses to pass through to the owners as income on their personal tax returns," Brian Cairns, CEO of ProStrategix Consulting, explained. "LLCs can have one or more members, and revenues and losses do not have to be shared equally."

The state filing fee, which can range from $40 to $500 depending on the state, is included in the cost of incorporating an LLC. The state of New York, for example, charges a $200 registration fee and a $9 biennial cost for forming an LLC. You must also file a biannual statement with the New York State Department of State.

Despite the fact that small firms can form LLCs, some huge corporations do so. Anheuser-Busch Companies, one of the largest beer companies in the United States, is an example of an LLC.

Examples of limited liability companies (LLCs)

The LLC is commonly used by accounting, tax, and law firms, but it can also be used by other sorts of businesses.

Well-known examples include:

- Pepsi-Cola
- Sony
- Nike
- Hertz Rent-a-Car
- eBay
- IBM

4. Corporation

A corporation is treated by the law as a separate entity from its owners. It possesses legal rights independent of its owners, including the ability to sue and be sued, acquire and sell property, and sell ownership rights in the form of stocks. Fees for forming a corporation differ by state and charge category. The S corporation and C corporation costs in New York, for example, are $130, while the nonprofit fee is $75.

Companies can be classified as C corporations, S corporations, B corporations, closed corporations, or nonprofit corporations.

C corporations, which are owned by shareholders, are taxed separately. Morgan Chase & Co. is a C corporation that is a multinational investment bank and financial services holding business. Many larger organizations, such as Apple Inc., Bank of America, and Amazon, apply for C corporations because they allow an unlimited number of stockholders.

S corporations, like partnerships and LLCs, were created for small enterprises to avoid double taxation. Owners are also only covered for a limited amount of responsibility. Widgets Inc. is an example of a straightforward S corporation:

employee salaries are subject to FICA tax, but further profits distributed by the S corporation are not subject to additional FICA tax.

B corporations, often known as benefit corporations, are for-profit businesses that aim to have a beneficial social impact. The Body Shop has earned B corporation accreditation after demonstrating a long-term commitment to environmental and social causes. The Body Shop uses its presence to fight for long-term change on topics such as human trafficking, domestic abuse, climate change, deforestation, and cosmetic industry animal experimentation.

Closed corporations are not publicly traded and have minimal liability protection. They are typically operated by a few stockholders. Closed corporations, sometimes known as privately held firms, offer more flexibility than publicly traded corporations. Hobby Lobby is a privately held, family-owned company that operates as a closed corporation. Hobby Lobby equities aren't traded on the open market; instead, they've been allotted to family members.

On a public market, open corporations can be traded. Many well-known businesses, such as Microsoft and Ford Motor Company, operate as open organizations. Each entity has taken control of the business and is now open to investment from anyone.

Nonprofit organizations exist to assist others in some capacity, and they are rewarded with tax exemption. The Salvation Army, the American Heart Association, and the American Red Cross are examples of nonprofits. The main goal of these sorts of business arrangements is to focus on something other than making a profit.

The following are some of the benefits of this firm structure:

Liability is limited. Stockholders are only accountable for their personal investments and are not personally liable for claims against your company.

Continuity. Death or the transfer of shares by shareholders has no effect on corporations. Investors, creditors, and customers prefer that your firm continues to run indefinitely.

Capital. When your company is incorporated, it is considerably easier to raise huge amounts of money from various investors.

Rather than a startup based in a living room, this form of company is suitable for businesses that are farther along in their growth. For example, if you've founded a shoe company and have already given it a name, selected directors, and secured funds from investors, the next step is to incorporate. You're basically doing business at a higher-risk, higher-reward rate. Additionally, your company could file as a S corporation to take advantage of the tax benefits that come with it.

Corporations as examples;

It's probably in your best interest to incorporate your business once it reaches a particular size.

There are numerous well-known examples of corporations, such as:

- General Motors
- Amazon
- Exxon Mobil
- Domino's Pizza

- P. Morgan Chase

5. Cooperative

A cooperative (co-op) is a company that is owned and operated by the people it serves. Its services benefit the company's members, also known as user-owners, who vote on the mission and direction of the organization and share earnings. Cooperatives have the following benefits:

Reduced taxes. A cooperative, like an LLC, does not tax its members' earnings.

Funding has been increased. Federal grants may be available to help cooperatives get founded.

Discounts and improved service are available. Cooperatives can make use of their scale to get discounts on goods and services for their members.

Choosing a nonprofit organization name that specifies whether the cooperative is a corporation, such as incorporated (Inc.) or limited, is a difficult task. The cost of registering a co-op agreement varies by state. The filing charge for an incorporated business in New York, for example, is $125.

CHS Inc., a Fortune 100 company owned by agricultural cooperatives in the United States, is an example of a co-op. CHS, the country's largest agribusiness cooperative, has recorded a net income of $829.9 million for the fiscal year that ended on August 31, 2019.

Cooperatives as examples

Co-ops, unlike other forms of enterprises, are owned by the individuals who use them.

Co-ops include the following notable examples:

- Land O'Lakes
- Navy Federal Credit Union
- Welch's
- REI
- Ace Hardware

The sole proprietorship, partnership, Limited Liability Company, corporation, and cooperative are the five forms of business structures. The structure you choose is largely determined by the nature of your firm. You'll be able to change structures as your company expands to fit its needs.

Consider these factors before deciding on a nonprofit organization structure

It's not always straightforward to pick which structure to use for new enterprises that fall into two or more of these categories. You should think about your startup's financial demands, risk, and growth potential. It can be tough to change your legal structure after you've registered your company, so think about it carefully when you're first starting out.

Here are some crucial things to think about while deciding on a legal structure for your company. You should also schedule a meeting with your CPA to seek his or her counsel.

Flexibility

Where do you see your company going, and what kind of legal structure will allow it to expand the way you want it to? Review your goals in your business strategy and choose which structure best suits those aims. Your organization should foster the prospect of development and change rather than stifle it.

Complexity

Nothing beats a sole proprietorship when it comes to starting and operational complexity. You simply register your business name, begin doing business, record your profits, and pay personal income taxes on it. Outside funding, on the other hand, can be difficult to come by. Partnerships, on the other hand, necessitate a formal agreement that spells out the duties and profit splits. State governments and the federal government have different reporting obligations for corporations and limited liability companies.

Liability

Because it is its own legal entity, a corporation carries the least level of personal culpability. This means that creditors and consumers can sue the company, but they won't be able to seize the officials' or shareholders' personal assets. An LLC provides the same level of protection as a sole proprietorship while also providing tax benefits. Partnerships divide liabilities among the partners according to the terms of their partnership agreement.

Taxation

An LLC owner pays taxes in the same way that a sole proprietor does: all profits are treated as personal income and taxed as such at the end of the year.

"You want to avoid double taxes as a nonprofit organization owner in the early stages," Jennifer Friedman, chief marketing expert at Expertly.com, stated. "The LLC structure prohibits this and ensures that you are taxed as an individual rather than a corporation."

Individuals who are part of a partnership can claim their share of the profits as personal income as well. To minimize the end effect on your return, your accountant may recommend quarterly or biannual advance payments.

Each year, a corporation files its own tax returns, paying taxes on profits after deducting expenses such as wages. If you receive compensation from the corporation, you must pay personal taxes on your personal return, such as Social Security and Medicare.

Control

A sole proprietorship or an LLC may be the best option for you if you want sole or principal control over your nonprofit organization and its activities. Control can also be negotiated in a cooperation agreement.

A corporation is designed to have a board of directors that makes the company's important decisions. A single individual can oversee a corporation, especially at its birth, but as it grows, the requirement for it to be run by a board of directors grows as well. The regulations designed for larger companies

– such as keeping track of every key action that affects the company – nevertheless apply to small nonprofit organizations.

Investment in capital

If you need outside finance, such as from an investor, venture capitalist, or bank, forming a corporation may be a preferable option. Corporations are more likely than sole proprietorships to be able to seek outside finance.

Corporations can sell stock to raise money for expansion, but sole proprietors can only get money from their own accounts, personal credit, or by bringing in partners. An LLC can suffer comparable challenges, albeit because it is its own business, the owner does not always need to use their own credit or assets.

Regulations, licenses, and permits

You may require particular licenses and permits to operate in addition to officially registering your nonprofit entity. Depending on the sort of business and its activity, local, state, and federal licenses may be required.

Friedman explained that "states have various criteria for different company models." "There may be varying restrictions at the municipal level depending on where you start your shop. Understand the state and industry you're in when you choose your structure. It isn't a 'one-size-fits-all' solution, and firms may be unaware of what is relevant to them."

Only for-profit businesses are covered by the structures outlined here. Friedman recommends contacting a business law consultant if you've done your studies and still aren't sure which company structure is best for you.

Essentials tools for Nonprofit Organization

Nonprofit organizations must make use of the technologies available to guarantee that their operations are streamlined. These are:

- Social Media Platforms
- Business email
- Business Phone
- Business Zoom
- Business Bank Accounts

Resources

<u>Burst</u> — this free photo site, powered by Spotify, has hundreds of images for commercial and personal use.

<u>Shutterstock</u> - Shutter stock is the most comprehensive option, selling photographs, images, videos, and music.

<u>Pexels</u> – These royalty-free and attribution-free pictures can be used anywhere.

One of our favorite online image editors is <u>Canva</u>. You can quickly edit images, but you can also create a wide range of visuals, including posters, business cards, and book covers. The basic version is free, and if you require more features, you may upgrade to the "work" edition.

<u>Kickstarter</u> is a United States-based global crowdsourcing website. The company's stated aim is to assist in the realization of creative ideas. Kickstarter funding is all-or-nothing. A pledge to a project will not be charged until it reaches its financing target.

<u>Maestro Label Designer</u> — this free web-based tool provides label users with customized design and printing possibilities.

<u>The Print Shop</u> - This CD program, which is a nonprofit organization partner, will help you develop brochures, labels, newsletters, and more.

Boardable :: <u>boardable.com</u>

Boardable enables boards and committees to easily schedule, meet, and collaborate virtually or in person.

GrantAdvisor :: *grantadvisor.org*

GrantAdvisor allows anyone in the nonprofit community to anonymously write reviews about their grant experiences with foundations.

Idealist.org :: *idealist.org*

Idealist.org is the world's leading platform for nonprofit jobs and volunteer opportunities.

NetSquared :: *netsquared.org*

NetSquared is a group of volunteer leaders who host free #TechforGood in-person events every month in 120 cities worldwide.

Open Data Project :: *nptechforgood.com/open-data-project*

Based on survey data from charitable organizations worldwide, the Open Data Project illuminates how nonprofits, NGOs, and charities worldwide use technology for digital marketing and fundraising.

Shopify Nonprofit Program :: *shopify.com/nonprofit*

Shopify allows nonprofits to develop an online storefront at a discounted rate so your charity or nonprofit can sell products online.

Timecounts :: *timecounts.org*

Timecounts is an online volunteer program management program that empowers nonprofits to easily recruit, manage and mobilize volunteers.

TechSoup :: *techsoup.org*

TechSoup has partnered with technology companies and organizations to offer heavily discounted software to organizations worldwide.

Postable :: *postable.com*

Postable allows users to easily send cards and postcards through snail mail. Ideal for thanking donors, volunteers, and supporters.

Chapter Six - Business Plan the Secret Weapon!

Planning for nonprofit organization success

When you're running a nonprofit organization, it's easy to get caught up in the details and lose sight of the greater picture. Successful nonprofit organizations, on the other hand, devote effort to developing and managing budgets, preparing and reviewing company plans, and routinely monitoring finances and performance.

Structured planning can make all the difference in your company's growth. It will allow you to focus your efforts on boosting earnings, lowering costs, and enhancing returns on investment.

Many organizations, in reality, carry out the majority of the activities connected with nonprofit planning, such as thinking about growth areas, competition, cash flow, and profit, even if they don't have a formal process in place.

It doesn't have to be complicated or time-consuming to turn this into a unified method for managing your company's growth. The most important thing is that plans are developed, that they are dynamic, and that everyone involved is aware of them. See the page on what to include in your annual plan in this handbook.

The advantages

The main advantage of nonprofit organization planning is that it allows you to focus on the path of your company and sets goals that will help it expand. It will also allow you to take a step back and assess your performance as well as the issues affecting your company. Nonprofit organization planning can provide you with the following benefits:

- A better ability to make continuous improvements and foresee issues.
- Dependable financial data on which to make decisions.
- Enhanced attention and clarity
- A boost in your decision-making confidence

Budgeting and planning in nonprofit organization

The effectiveness of a nonprofit owner's planning process is critical to the success of a small firm. Nonprofit budget planning, which is also one of the final stages of the planning process, is one of the most important components of the planning process. To begin, gather financial data, predictions, and industry analysis to aid in the development of your nonprofit budget.

It's critical to plan and closely manage your company's financial success after it's up and running. The most effective approach to keeping your firm--and its money - on track is to establish a budgeting procedure.

This section describes how to plan and budget for your nonprofit organization and the benefits of doing so. It includes action items to assist you better manage your company's finances and make sure your plans are feasible.

Budgeting and strategic planning

Nonprofit organization owners who are just starting out may not realize the importance of budgeting. You will, however, need to fund your plans if you are planning for the future of your company. Budgeting is the most effective strategy to keep track of your financial flow and invest in new prospects when the timing is right.

You may not always be able to be hands-on with every aspect of your nonprofit organization as it grows. You may need to divide your budget among many departments, such as sales, production, and marketing. You'll notice that money starts to flow in a variety of places throughout your company; budgets are a critical tool for staying in control of spending.

A budget is a strategy for:

- Keep financial control
- Make sure you'll be able to meet your current obligations.
- This empowers you to make sound financial decisions and achieve your goals.
- Ensure that you have sufficient funds for future projects.

It lays out how you plan to spend your money and how you plan to pay for it. It is not, however, a prediction. A forecast is a prediction of the future, whereas a budget is a planned outcome of the future, determined by your company strategy.

The Advantages Of A Nonprofit Organization Budget

Drawing up a nonprofit organization budget has a lot of advantages, including being better prepared to:

- Efficiently handle your finances
- Projects should be given adequate resources.
- Keep an eye on things.
- You achieve your goals.
- Better decision-making
- Identify issues before they arise, such as the need for more funding or cash flow issues.
- Make a future plan
- Boost employee motivation.

Making a financial plan

The ability to create, monitor, and manage a budget is critical to a company's success. It should assist you in allocating resources where they are needed to keep your company profitable and successful. It doesn't have to be difficult. All you have to do now is figure out how much money you'll make and how much money you'll spend over the budget period.

What Exactly Is Nonprofit Organization Capital, And Why Is It So Crucial?

Nonprofit organization capital is an accounting phrase that you may not hear much about, but it could be the key to your company's success. Nonprofit organization capital has an impact on many elements of your organization, including paying staff and vendors, keeping the lights on, and planning for long-term growth. In a nutshell, working capital is the cash on hand to cover immediate, short-term obligations.

To make sure your nonprofit capital is working for you, you'll need to figure out what you have now, anticipate what you'll need in the future, and think about how to make sure you always have enough cash.

What is the formula for nonprofit organization capital?

Determine your working capital ratio, a gauge of your company's short-term financial health, to get a sense of where you are right now.

The formula for calculating nonprofit organization capital:

Current assets / current liabilities = working capital ratio.

Your working capital ratio is 2:1 if you have $1 million in current assets and $500,000 in current liabilities. Although a ratio of 1.2:1 is generally considered healthy, in some industries or types of enterprises, a ratio as low as 1.2:1 may be sufficient.

Your net working capital indicates how much cash you have on hand to cover current expenses.

The formula for net business capital:

Net working capital equals current assets less current liabilities.

Only short-term assets such as cash in your business account, accounts receivable (money owed to you by customers), and inventory that you anticipate to convert to cash within 12 months are considered in these calculations.

Accounts payable, which is money you owe vendors and other creditors, as well as other obligations and accumulated expenses for payroll, taxes, and other outlays, are all examples of short-term liabilities.

Recognizing your requirements

Plotting month-by-month inflows and outflows for your firm will help you get a better grasp of your working capital requirements. For example, a landscaping company's revenues may peak in the spring, then remain pretty stable through October, before plummeting to nearly zero in the late fall and winter. On the other hand, the company may have a large number of ongoing expenses throughout the year.

Parts of these computations may necessitate making educated estimates about what will happen in the future. While historical results might help, you'll also need to account for future contracts you plan to sign and the potential loss of key customers. Making accurate estimates might be especially difficult if your company is rapidly expanding.

These estimates can help you figure out which months have more money going out than coming in, and which months have the largest cash flow gap.

There Are Four Reasons Why Your Nonprofit Organization Could Need More Operating Capital

Seasonal variations in cash flow are common in many firms, which may require additional capital to prepare for a busy season or to keep the business running when revenue is low.

While waiting for payments from clients, almost every nonprofit will require additional working capital to meet obligations to suppliers, employees, and the government.

Extra working cash can benefit your nonprofit organization in a variety of ways, such as allowing you to take advantage of supplier discounts by purchasing in quantity.

Working capital can also be used to pay for temporary workers or other project-related costs.

Looking for ways to increase your nonprofit organization capital?

An unsecured revolving line of credit can be a good way to boost your operating capital. Lines of credit are meant to support temporary working capital needs, have better terms than business credit cards, and allow your company to draw only what it needs when it needs it.

While a company credit card can be a convenient way for you and your top employees to handle incidental expenses such as travel, entertainment, and other necessities, it is rarely the greatest answer for working capital. Increased interest rates, higher costs for cash advances, and the ease with which one might accumulate excessive debt are all limitations.

Obtaining a line of credit for nonprofit capital

Lenders will assess the overall health of your balance sheet, including your working capital ratio, net working capital, annual revenue, and other indicators when you apply for a line of credit. See what banks are looking for in businesses that are looking for funding.

Lenders will look at your personal financial accounts, credit score, and tax returns because small company owners' business and personal affairs are often connected. A personal guarantee of repayment will be required.

Although a variety of factors influence the size of your working capital line of credit, a general rule of thumb is that it should not exceed 10% of your company's revenues.

What Is The Significance Of Nonprofit Organization Accounting?

Accounting is critical for nonprofit organization owners because it allows owners, managers, investors, and other stakeholders to assess the company's financial success. Accounting provides crucial information about costs and profits, profit and loss, liabilities and assets for decision-making, planning, and control activities inside a company.

Accounting's basic goal is to record financial transactions in books of accounts in order to identify, quantify, and transmit economic data. Furthermore, tax reporting companies need you to keep basic books that document income and expenses.

What Is the Importance of Accounting?

Accounting is essential to running a nonprofit organization because it allows you to track income and expenses, maintain statutory compliance, and offer quantifiable financial information to investors, management, and the government that can be used to make nonprofit choices.

Your records generate three important financial statements.

The income statement tells you how much money you made and how much money you lost.

The balance sheet gives you a clear view of your company's financial situation on a specific day.

The cash flow statement is a link between the income statement and the balance sheet that shows how much money was made and spent over a period of time.

If you want to keep your nonprofit organization afloat, you must keep your financial records clean and up to date. Here are a few of the reasons why it is critical for your company, no matter how big or little!

It aids in the evaluation of nonprofit organization performance.

Your financial records represent the financial situation of your nonprofit organization or corporation as well as the results of operations. In other words, they assist you in gaining a better understanding of your company's financial situation. Clean and current records will not only help you keep track of spending, gross margin, and potential debt, but they will also allow you to compare current data to past accounting records and allocate your budget accordingly.

It ensures that the law is followed.

Although state laws and regulations differ, efficient accounting systems and processes will assist you in ensuring statutory compliance in your organization.

Liabilities such as sales tax, VAT, income tax, and pension funds, to name a few, will be treated effectively by the accounting department.

It assists in the creation of budgets and future projections.

Budgeting and future estimates can make or break a company, and your financial records will be critical in this regard.

To keep your operations profitable, nonprofit trends and estimates are based on previous financial data. This financial data is most useful when it comes from well-organized accounting operations.

It aids in the preparation of financial statements.

The Registrar of Companies requires nonprofit organizations to file their financial statements. Listed companies must submit them to stock exchanges as well as to the IRS for direct and indirect tax purposes. Accounting, of course, plays a crucial part in all of these instances.

The Importance of Filing a nonprofit Income Tax Return

Your success in life is measured in numbers: the numbers in your bank account and the annual profits reported on your tax return. These figures can either open or close doors, providing opportunities for progress and growth. By filing their annual income tax return, nonprofit organization owners and professionals will receive extra opportunities. Filing your income tax return has two purposes: it not only allows you to declare your earnings to the IRS and pay any taxes owed, but it also allows you to take advantage of various perks that will benefit you in the short and long term. Let's take a look at the advantages of filing your taxes as a nonprofit organization owner or professional.

Filing a Tax Return Has Many Advantages for nonprofit organizations and Professionals

Losses are carried forward.

Losses are unavoidable in the corporate world. If you have capital losses, you can deduct them from your income under the category "Profit and Gains of Business and Profession." You can carry over your losses for up to 8 years if you file an income tax return. This option to carry forward losses, however, is only available if your annual tax return is filed. This implies you can carry over past losses to offset future gains in succeeding years to minimize the amount of taxes you owe.

92

Request a loan

Organizations, like individuals, require loans at various times in their lives. Loans are commonly used by organizations to expand and enhance their operations. When requesting for a loan at a critical stage in your organization's growth, your income tax return is a vital document that banks will want, among other things, before assessing if your nonprofit organization is a sound investment for them to award a substantial quantity of money that you should be able to repay. So, completing your income tax return on time, every year, provides benefits that will benefit you in several aspects of building your firm.

Avoids Punishment and Prosecution

Tax evasion is punishable severely all around the world, especially in India. Late filing also comes with fines, which might eat into your profits. As a result, timely filing of your income tax returns will spare you from avoidable tough situations with the IRS, allowing you to focus on your organization in peace.

Obtain Tenders from the Government

Your organization's financial situation and achievements are reflected in your income tax returns. The successful verification of your financial records, which is done by verifying your annual tax returns for the last many years, is typically linked to the acquisition of government tenders. Cross-checking will be done on the applicant who is most suited for the tender to see if he or she is capable of overseeing the project. Professionals who want to land contracts should make sure their company tax returns are completed on time and precisely, as an audit may be required, just as it is for enterprises.

Depreciation Claim

According to income tax legislation, assets in the name of the firm or owner allow you to claim depreciation. The asset being claimed, however, must be used solely for the purposes of the business or profession. If you haven't chosen the Presumptive Taxation Scheme, you can compute your total taxable earnings by subtracting all expenses and depreciation allowed under section 32 of the income tax act. As a result, by preparing your tax returns, you may optimize your profits by taking advantage of all available deductions, such as depreciation.

Take advantage of the Presumptive Taxation Scheme.

Under the Presumptive Taxation Scheme under section 44AD, the Income Tax Department permits small enterprises and professionals to pay tax on only a percentage of their earnings, easing the burden of paying taxes. This scheme is available to professionals earning less than Rs 50 lakh and enterprises generating less than Rs 2 crore. Professionals are only required to pay taxes on 50% of their profits, whereas corporations are only required to pay taxes on 8% of their earnings. To take advantage of the benefits of this program, taxpayers must file ITR 4 tax returns.

Every person's ambition is to develop and grow. This expansion extends into the careers of enterprises and professionals. Filing your tax return on time each year can open doors to help you realize your ambitions of success and prosperity.

The Importance of POS (Point-of-Sale) Systems for nonprofit organization

Today, POS systems are becoming more popular, and here are the top six reasons why firms choose to invest in one:

1. Sales Reports

A POS system provides you with a comprehensive view of your company and automatically tracks its cash flow. It is simple to find information about a product line.

Another advantage of a POS system is the ability to save information about your financial situation, inventory situation, and sales situation. You can plan the revenue that would be statistically expected for the month, the next two months, or the coming week based on this information.

Fill out the form on this page for a personal consultation on the best POS system for your business, and we will contact you. Our service is provided without charge.

2. Change Product Offers

Advanced reports can clearly show which product categories are the most profitable and which are the least profitable. Knowing which departments and items are underperforming might help you design a sales plan. As a result, based on your industry, you can adapt your store items, menu, and much more.

In addition, the system generates in-depth analysis of customers' purchasing habits on its own. This POS system feature will enable your organization to adjust to the needs of the group without the need for costly hours of research.

3. Save time

Another advantage of a POS system is that it allows you to keep track of deliveries and all goods leaving your store. The system keeps track of how much a certain product has sold and keeps you up to date on what you have in stock. When the inventory is nearly depleted, the POS system can submit orders to the suppliers on its own. As a result, there is no need for an employee to devote time to it.

When a buyer requests information on a certain product, the seller can immediately look it up in the program. Reducing the amount of time a customer has to wait will improve the level of service you can provide.

A POS system can also assist you with automatically defining margins and calculating taxes. Everyday chores for your staff will become easier and faster, whether they use stationary or mobile POS systems.

4. Reduce errors as much as possible

A product's price can be adjusted, and it will be updated throughout the system, ensuring that prices remain consistent throughout the process. As a result, the corporation ensures that prices always match the price quoted to the consumer in order to avoid unsatisfied customers.

5. Customer Loyalty Program

A POS system can save all of your customer information, allowing you to provide outstanding customer care to your loyal customers. In fact, it enables you to determine which of your consumers' favorite products are. When you customize your product offers and promotions for each of your consumers, this feature of POS systems can be really handy. They will feel special and well cared for, which may lead to a purchasing decision.

6. Management of Employees

A point-of-sale system can be used to track each employee's additional sales. It can, however, be utilized as a management tool and a reward criterion. Employees will be more motivated and effective as a result of this. As a result, revenues will rise and customer service will improve.

On the other side, the employee can review his or her own sales figures, which can aid in the employee's understanding of his or her own personal goals. It also allows them to see where they can enhance the numbers.

To recap, a POS system helps your firm become more cost-conscious, provides you a better understanding of revenues, saves time, enhances client relations, and uses previously collected data to develop economic targets.

How to Start a Nonprofit Organization

How Long Does It Take to Form a Nonprofit Organization?

Forming a nonprofit will take at least six months from a legal standpoint. If you're starting from scratch, it could take anything from 12 to 18 months (for example, you have no clue who could possibly be a member of your board yet).

Starting a Nonprofit Organization

We'd like to be clear right away that we're not attorneys or accountants. While we are knowledgeable about the nonprofit creation process and principles, we urge that you consult with an attorney and an accountant to assure compliance. There are tools and templates available to assist you with this process on your own, but you'd be taking a risk if you didn't seek competent legal advice or guidance to ensure your organization complies with your state's nonprofit laws.

Carry out your research

Make a point of saving any qualitative and quantitative data you collect throughout the study process. It will undoubtedly come in helpful as "base data" when you begin monitoring and assessing the activities of your business in the future. After all, you need to know what the playing field was like when you first started to quantify your influence!

Determine the Demand

Before you begin your plans and activities, make sure that what you're doing is a viable solution to the problem you've identified.

If you're considering founding a new nonprofit, make sure the work you'll be doing meets an existing need before you put your time and money into it. As humans, we have a natural desire to help others, but it is vital to use this inclination wisely, determining what needs people have and how those needs might be effectively met.

Let's look at some statistics from the nonprofit industry. In the United States, there are 1.5 million NGOs registered, 45,000 of which help veterans and 3,500 of which are animal shelters.

It's critical to consider how your activity complements that of other organizations currently in existence. After all, collaborating rather than starting from scratch may be the best option. You don't want to waste time, money, or effort trying to recreate the wheel.

It's also a good idea to check out what other nonprofits are registered in your county, state, or region to see whether any of them compete directly with the job you want to accomplish. While it may seem strange to consider NGOs competing, it is a reality and a necessary step.

Remember that competition isn't always a negative thing—partnering with an existing organization or structuring your nonprofit to provide complementary services to those that currently exist could help you make a bigger impact on the topic you care about. Identifying where your nonprofit fits into the existing ecosystem will only increase the likelihood of your effect being successful.

Completing a Needs Assessment for the community or region you wish to serve is a fantastic approach to thinking about your nonprofit in this context.

Resources

Quickbooks produced this sales tax rates tool to assist nonprofit organization owners in determining the appropriate sales tax rates. Your tax calculator will do it for you for free if you use Quickbooks or TurboTax.

SalesForce — with practically everything integrated, Sales Force is able to give intelligent reporting.

Quickbooks — this software can generate basic and custom reports, giving you a complete picture of your company.

Pipedrive — rather than waiting for reports, see your sales in real time with Pipedrive.

Monday.com - this organizational tool allows you to track your business in a customizable method.

Zendesk Sell — with sales forecasting tools and prediction capabilities, the future is now.

MailChimp Marketing CRM — this all-in-one marketing tool may assist you in gathering data, organizing it, and even automating some of your tasks.

Copify :: *copify.com*

Copify is a portal to copywriters for hire. For $.06 a word, your nonprofit can hire professional writers for your website, blog content, and reports.

EventBrite :: *eventbrite.com*

Eventbrite enables users to create professional event ticketing and registration pages.

Skedulo :: *skedulo.com*

Skedulo empowers nonprofits to manage the schedules of a hybrid workforce.

Gusto :: *gusto.com*

Gusto is an affordable solution for managing payroll, benefits, and HR.

MeetUp :: *meetup.com*

MeetUp is a service that focuses on helping people meet up offline and in person. For small regional nonprofits, the service could be used for local events and regular meetups.

Upwork :: *upwork.com*

From programmers to designers, Upwork enables you to easily hire skilled freelancers. You can upload projects, receive bids, and browse examples of completed work.

Timecounts :: *timecounts.org*

Timecounts is an online volunteer program management program that empowers nonprofits to easily recruit, manage and mobilize volunteers.

TechSoup :: *techsoup.org*

TechSoup has partnered with technology companies and organizations to offer heavily discounted software to organizations worldwide.

VolunteerMatch :: *volunteermatch.org*

VolunteerMatch is an online portal to volunteer opportunities posted by over 100K nonprofits.

Conclusion

Prepare a strategic plan

It will be vital to develop a strategic plan for how your organization will run, execute its goals, hire people, and grow. It will be difficult to ensure the success of your organization without a strategic strategy in place. Strategic plans are blueprints that you may refer to over and over to ensure that your nonprofit is on the right road. Look for an excellent resource or guidebook that outlines how to create a strategic strategy for your nonprofit.

Consider the long term

Hopefully, your nonprofit will be successful for the rest of your life and beyond. Keep this long-term vision in mind as you start your nonprofit. Rather than haphazardly putting your company together, it is vital to create a solid basis from the start. Consider devoting six to a year at the start to develop a solid fund-raising foundation, great programs, and best practices. Use the first year, for example, to fundraise and generate awareness for your organization so that you can stick to your budget. Then, with stable revenue, you can focus on paying personnel, covering office expenditures, and funding projects. Once your programs begin, it will become increasingly difficult to devote 100 percent of your efforts to fundraising.

Have a good time

It should be enjoyable to assist people. It can be enjoyable to start and maintain a successful nonprofit. If you lose the "fun element" at any moment, regroup and figure out how to reintroduce it to your efforts. It will be tough to keep going if fun and happiness are not a consistent component of your charitable operations. Make sure the people you're helping, the volunteers, and yourself are having a good time, and your organization will thrive.

Passion

Remember why you started your nonprofit in the first place: to make a difference in the world, not to enrich yourself. Running a nonprofit requires both a passion for making a difference in the world and the ability to make that desire a reality.

www.ingramcontent.com/pod-product-compliance
Lightning Source LLC
Chambersburg PA
CBHW052051270326
41931CB00012B/2715